THE SCIENCE OF A TSUNAMI

ROBIN KOONTZ

Published in the United States of America
by Cherry Lake Publishing
Ann Arbor, Michigan
www.cherrylakepublishing.com

Consultants: Stephen A. Nelson, Associate Professor of Earth and Environmental Sciences, Tulane University;
Marla Conn, ReadAbility, Inc.
Editorial direction: Red Line Editorial
Book production: Design Lab
Book design: Sleeping Bear Press

Photo Credits: Kyodo News/AP Images, cover, 1, 12; J. David Long/iStockphoto, 5; Deddeda Stemler/Canadian Press/AP
Images, 7; iStockphoto, 9, 19, 21; E. Glanfield/Shutterstock Images, 15; Andersen Oystein/iStockphoto, 16; Rick Bowmer/
AP Images, 22; David Butow/Corbis, 25; Marco Garcia/AP Images, 28

Library of Congress Cataloging-in-Publication Data
  CIP data has been filed and is available at catalog.loc.gov.

Cherry Lake Publishing would like to acknowledge the work of
the Partnership for 21st Century Skills. Please visit *www.p21.org*
for more information.

Printed in the United States of America
Corporate Graphics
June 2015

ABOUT THE AUTHOR

Robin Koontz is an author and illustrator of books, educational blogs, and articles for children and
young adults. Her 2011 book *Leaps and Creeps: How Animals Move to Survive* was an Animal
Behavior Society Outstanding Children's Book Award Finalist. Raised in Maryland and Alabama,
Koontz now lives with her husband in western Oregon.

TABLE OF CONTENTS

CHAPTER 1

KILLER WAVE

It was the morning of December 26, 2004. While life went on as usual, one of the largest tsunamis in history was about to hit the Sumatra region of western Indonesia.

In coastal areas, people were working or relaxing along the beaches. They saw that the ocean water was moving rapidly away from the shore. Many were amazed by the sight. Some tourists ran closer to take pictures. They did not know about the dangerous event that would soon take place.

Minutes later, a massive wave approached the beach. The water surged past the shoreline, crashing through buildings, trees, and cars. People ran to higher places to escape. Some clung to trees. Others tried to hold on to floating debris in the water. But for many, it was too late. They were caught in the deadly tsunami.

The tsunami hit Banda Aceh, a city in Sumatra, Indonesia.

Tsunami is a Japanese word from *tsu* (harbor) and *nami* (wave). Many tsunamis are caused by underwater earthquakes. On that day in 2004, a massive earthquake occurred in the Indian Ocean. After the earthquake, Northern Sumatra and the Nicobar Islands were the first places struck by a giant wave. For the next several hours, devastating tsunami waves struck many other countries around the Indian Ocean. Waves traveled more than

THE WORLDWIDE EFFECTS OF TSUNAMIS

A powerful earthquake caused a tsunami to sweep over the east coast of Japan in 2011. The tsunami damaged many coastal homes and communities. The same earthquake caused tsunami waves to hit areas in California, Oregon, and Hawaii. The tsunami also caused large slabs of ice to break from ice shelves in Antarctica. Tsunamis can affect areas thousands of miles away.

People in Thailand surveyed the damage from the 2004 tsunami.

3,000 miles (5,000 km) to crash onto the coasts of southern India and East Africa.

When the destructive event was finally over, it had affected 14 different countries in South Asia and East Africa. Nearly 300,000 people were killed or missing. The waves had destroyed buildings, bridges, and roads. Hundreds of thousands of people were left homeless. Entire islands were gone. It was the worst tsunami event in recorded history.

— CHAPTER 2 —

EARTHQUAKES AND TSUNAMIS

In an underwater earthquake, the seafloor suddenly moves up or down. The movement of the seafloor **displaces** the overlying water. Waves rapidly spread in all directions. A tsunami wave can reach a speed of more than 500 miles per hour (805 kmh). Imagine a wave traveling as fast as a jet airplane. That's how fast a tsunami can roar through the ocean. It can travel thousands of miles in just a few hours.

How do these underwater earthquakes happen? The **tectonic** plates that make up Earth's crust press against

8

one another. These plates shift, push, and often build up pressure. Sometimes the pressure is released. That release of energy causes an earthquake.

Before the 2004 tsunami in the Indian Ocean, two tectonic plates that had been stuck together for many years suddenly broke free. The plate movement caused trillions of tons of rock to shift. As a result, the ground shuddered violently. The earthquake caused the seafloor to lift up, displacing the water. Massive waves formed.

Earth consists of four layers. The top layer is the crust, made up of dirt and rocks. The crust is an average of 25 miles (40 km) thick, but it is thinner under the ocean. Under the crust, red-hot rocks make up the mantle. These

The layers of Earth, from outermost to innermost, include the crust, mantle, outer core, and inner core.

rocks can be so hot that they melt, creating a substance called **magma**. Under the mantle is the core of Earth. The outer core is made of liquid metal. The inner core is a solid mass of super-hot metals.

The crust makes up the surface of Earth. But the surface is not just a single solid mass. It contains many sections of different shapes and sizes. The sections, called plates, brush together, pull apart, and even collide. This movement is called plate tectonics. When

THREE KINDS OF TECTONIC BOUNDARIES

When edges of tectonic plates meet, they create different kinds of boundaries. Plates that crash into each other create a convergent plate boundary. Two plates that slide next to each other create a transform boundary. When plates pull apart, they create a divergent boundary. Along divergent boundaries, magma fills the gap between plates and cools to create new crust, which spreads along the seafloor.

HOW EARTHQUAKES FORM TSUNAMIS

A submarine earthquake releases energy. The arrows show energy from an earthquake that produces tsunami waves.

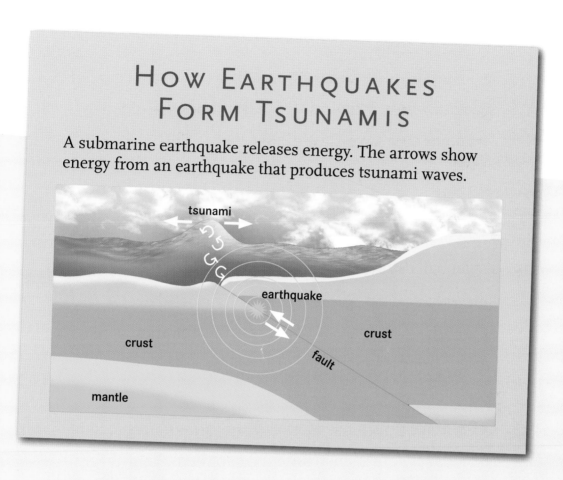

one plate slides under another, the area is called a **subduction zone**. Faults are fractures in the crust that form as a result.

Pieces of rocks break off as the tectonic plates move and rub together, creating rough edges. Sometimes plates get stuck together on the jagged edges, unable to

In 2011, waves swirled after a tsunami hit the northern coast of Japan.

move. They eventually become unstuck. The sudden release of energy as they move causes earthquakes.

Seismologists use tools called seismographs to study earthquakes. These instruments help them identify earthquakes that might cause tsunamis. Authorities use this information to warn people of possible tsunamis.

However, scientists cannot predict when earthquakes will happen. As a result, there is usually not much time to warn people about tsunami threats. Experts are working to increase warning times.

HOW SCIENCE WORKS
MODELING A TSUNAMI

In 2013, a large team collaborated on a project called the Science Application for Risk Reduction. The team of scientists and emergency experts put together a model of a tsunami that could be triggered by an earthquake near Alaska. Their goal was to study the impact this kind of tsunami could have on the California coast.

Scientists used evidence from past tsunamis, as well as knowledge of vulnerable areas. Then they identified the problems that the tsunami could cause. The scientists considered possible physical damage and evacuation challenges. They created the scenes that could happen if key ports and harbors were hit by a tsunami.

There may never be a tsunami event exactly like the scientists' model. But their conclusions will help them form plans for real disasters. Knowing more about what a tsunami could do will help response teams prepare for emergencies.

CHAPTER 3

VOLCANO AND LANDSLIDE TSUNAMIS

Earthquakes do not cause all tsunamis. Some types of tsunamis form due to volcanoes or landslides.

Volcanoes form near the edges of tectonic plates. When a subduction boundary is formed, the lower plate can move into the mantle. New magma forms, rising through passages of the volcano. Pressure builds and forces magma, ash, gas, and rocks through the passages. If enough pressure builds, the volcano erupts, and the materials can all burst to the surface. If the volcano is close to a coast, an avalanche of rocks and debris from the eruption can hit the water. The displacement of the water may form a tsunami wave.

One of the most destructive tsunamis ever recorded happened after the volcano Krakatau in Indonesia erupted in 1883. The tsunami waves triggered by the volcano destroyed entire towns and villages.

Krakatau continues to be an active volcano, with several recent eruptions.

Krakatau is located in the Ring of Fire, an area in the Pacific Ocean where volcanic eruptions, tsunamis, and earthquakes often occur. The Ring of Fire runs along the edges of the Pacific Plate. Volcanoes often reach above the ocean's surface, creating volcanic islands.

The most active volcanoes are hidden in the water, thousands of feet deep. The eruptions supply heat to

Powerful volcanic eruptions can send rocks and debris into the water.

THE LARGEST TSUNAMI WAVE EVER RECORDED

In 1958, an earthquake triggered a massive rockslide in southeast Alaska. The sudden impact of the rocks created a tsunami. The tsunami flooded the area and took down millions of trees. The wave reached a **run-up height** of approximately 1,720 feet (525 m). This kind of tsunami is sometimes called a splash wave. Objects that splash into the sea and displace water create splash waves.

underwater **ecosystems**. But underwater volcanoes can also cause tsunamis. Even worse, a volcano can trigger a landslide, creating even more potential for tsunami waves.

The movement of tectonic plates can create both earthquakes and volcanoes. Scientists are using underwater robots and submarines to study the thousands of underwater volcanoes in the Ring of Fire.

WHEN A TSUNAMI HITS LAND

Energy forms all waves. Different kinds of energy create different kinds of waves. Wind energy creates ocean waves. The pull of gravity from the Sun and Moon creates tidal waves.

Ocean waves and tidal waves are confined to the surface water. But a tsunami wave begins on the seafloor and affects water all the way up to the surface. As a result, it has a larger amount of energy than a normal wave. A tsunami wave also has a greater **wavelength**, giving it the strength to reach farther ashore.

[21ST CENTURY SKILLS LIBRARY]

Wind energy creates ocean waves.

Usually, a tsunami does not look like a typical breaking wave on the beach. It comes in like a fast-rising tide, traveling much farther than an ocean wave. The speed of a tsunami depends on the depth of the water. Tsunamis in deep water travel faster than tsunamis in shallower water.

The first tsunami wave may not be the only one, or even the worst one. Tsunami waves can hit the same area for many hours after the first wave arrives. A series of tsunami waves is called a wave train. In the open ocean, tsunami waves can be hard to detect. The waves can pile up when they reach shallow water, becoming even more powerful as the water surges up over the beach, over seawalls, and into villages and cities.

A tsunami wave might first appear as a shallow trough, which is the low point in front of the crest of the wave. It sucks water back and exposes the land. This sudden retreat of water is a common natural warning

How Tsunamis Form

1. Energy from a volcano, earthquake, or landslide suddenly displaces water.
2. The energy creates a train of waves that spread in widening circles.
3. The tsunami wavelengths grow, spreading farther apart.
4. Near a coastal land area, **friction** slows tsunamis down. The wavelengths get shorter, making the waves higher and more powerful.
5. The compressed wavelengths gain in height as they reach the shore. The powerful waves flood everything in their path.

A sign in Monterey, California, warns people of the risk of tsunamis.

sign of a tsunami. When people see this warning sign, they should leave the area. In only a few minutes, the wave's huge crest will hit the beach. People should also beware signs of earthquakes. If they notice that the ground is shaking, they should not wait for alarms or warnings. They should escape to higher ground as soon as possible.

Sometimes the tsunami loses energy when it runs into a bay, an entrance to a river, or structures in the water. But with nothing in its way, a tsunami can come

*At Oregon State University, scientists use a model of
a town near the ocean for tsunami experiments.*

in as a huge wave. It can also surge like a high tide gone
out of control, spreading farther and farther inland.
People have often said that a tsunami sounds like a
freight train. The energy in a tsunami can blast through
and destroy almost anything in its path.

Tsunamis can be triggered thousands of miles from
land and still create waves that can devastate large
landscapes. The tsunami that flooded Japan in 2011
swept a man in California out to sea. It also slammed
into Antarctica, more than 8,000 miles from Japan.

CASE STUDY
KICK'EM JENNY

Scientists and explorers are investigating a large underwater volcano in the Caribbean nicknamed Kick'em Jenny. They want to understand the earthquakes and tsunamis caused by underwater volcano eruptions. Kick'em Jenny is an active volcano in the Caribbean Sea. It is about 6,000 feet (1,830 m) below the surface.

Deep-sea explorer Robert Ballard set out to study the volcano and surrounding areas. Oceanographers and other explorers on the team used a remotely operated vehicle called Hercules. This underwater vehicle had no human crew but was armed with video cameras and audio equipment.

Hercules descended into the live volcano and reported back to a control room on the Nautilus, the team's ship. Hercules provided photographs and maps. It collected samples from inside the volcano's crater. It gathered hot ash and gas from dangerous areas. The photographs and samples will help scientists understand the dangers of an underwater eruption.

How Scientists Predict a Tsunami

Earthquakes, landslides, and volcano eruptions often happen in the ocean. Even if these events are not felt on land, they can create tsunamis that harm people.

How do scientists know if a tsunami is coming? In 1946, scientists started using the first tsunami warning system. They used tide gauges to detect tsunamis. Tide gauges are devices that measure changes in water height in areas of the ocean. The tide gauges helped scientists predict some tsunamis, but they could provide information only for the exact places where they were

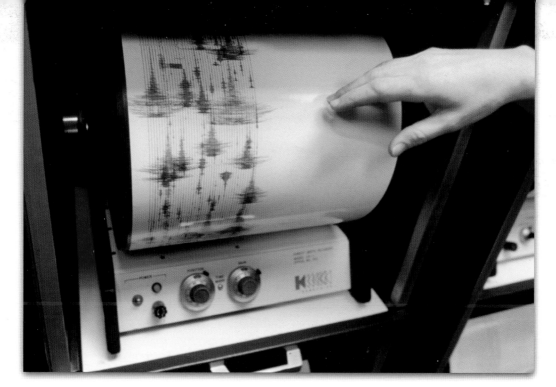

Scientists use instruments to record information about seismic waves.

located. Many false alarms were reported when tsunamis were too weak to cause any damage.

Today, there are better ways to identify a tsunami threat. Scientists use seismometers to detect earthquake action. Geologists who study plate tectonics can find where earthquakes are likely to occur. They use special sensors to detect movements in Earth's crust.

Scientists still use coastal tide gauges to watch for changes in sea level. But now they also have deep-ocean tsunami detection **buoy** systems that can observe changes

How People Escape Tsunamis

Sometimes people can escape tsunamis by noticing clues. The water in the ocean may pull far away from the shore. Or it may bubble and foam. Boats that are near the shore may bob up and down. Many beaches have signs to lead people to higher ground. Some areas also have sirens that blare if there is a tsunami alert. However, these warnings are often too late to be effective. If people notice signs of a tsunami, they should not wait for an official warning to escape.

in the sea level. A buoy system has a seabed detector on the ocean floor. This detector measures changes in the height of the water column by checking changes in water pressure. A buoy on the water surface receives information from the sensor and relays it to a satellite.

Satellites transmit this data to scientists at tsunami warning centers. A database helps the scientists compare information about changes in sea level with known tsunami characteristics. This helps them predict where tsunamis might go and how powerful the waves might become.

In 2004, there were only six modern buoy systems in place. None of them were in the Indian Ocean. Most communities in the area had no national warning centers. When the powerful tsunami hit Sumatra,

TSUNAMI BUOY DETECTION SYSTEM

This buoy on the ocean surface receives measurements of water level and pressure from an underwater instrument called a tsunameter. The buoy then sends this information to a satellite. The satellite sends the data to a tsunami warning center, where scientists study it.

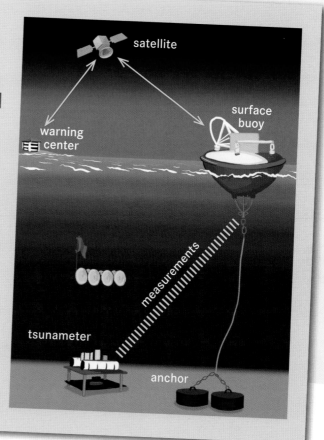

satellite

warning center

surface buoy

measurements

tsunameter

anchor

people in the area had only a few minutes to run. They were too close to the rupturing fault to escape. Two hours later, many thousands of people also perished in India. They did not know that the deadly tsunami was heading their way.

Now, most coastal areas around the world have warning systems to evacuate people if there is a

Scientists at the Pacific Tsunami Warning Center in Hawaii monitor conditions in the ocean.

How Science Works
A Tsunami Shield

In recent years, scientists have wondered if they could **deflect** waves. Engineer Sébastien Guenneau designed a structure to protect coastal areas from tsunamis. The structure is made of upright pillars. As a wave surges into the structure, the water is pushed left and right, turning the wave into a whirlpool. The energy is released in the structure instead of on land.

Building such a structure along a coastline would be a long, costly project. But Guenneau thinks it could work. The pillars would have little impact on the environment and could even become habitats for sea creatures.

tsunami alert. Once the buoy system detects an earthquake, scientists monitor the area for possible tsunamis. They know that in the ocean, a tsunami wave may seem to be a few inches above sea level. A passing boat might not even notice it. But the scientists know that more is going on deep in the water.

TOP FIVE
WORST TSUNAMIS

1. **Sumatra, Indonesia, December 26, 2004**
   An earthquake off the coast of Sumatra caused the most devastating tsunami in recorded history. The disaster damaged or destroyed coastal areas in 14 countries. As many as 300,000 people were killed.

2. **Lisbon, Portugal, November 1, 1755**
   An estimated 60,000 people were killed in Portugal, Morocco, and Spain after tsunami waves struck the coastal towns and villages. The massive waves were triggered by a powerful earthquake.

3. **Krakatau, Indonesia, August 27, 1883**
   When the Krakatau volcano exploded and collapsed, it triggered tsunami waves that traveled thousands of miles. An estimated 2,000 people were killed by the volcano. But about 38,000 perished because of the tsunami waves.

4. **Enshunada Sea, Japan, September 20, 1498**
   This tsunami wave was 56 feet (17 m) high, killing as many as 31,000 people. The tsunami was believed to be powerful enough to separate Lake Hamana from the sea.

5. **Japan, March 11, 2011**
   The north coast of Japan was slammed by a tsunami triggered by a massive earthquake in the Pacific Ocean. More than 18,000 people were killed.

LEARN MORE

FURTHER READING

Graham, Ian. *Tsunami: Perspectives on Tsunami Disasters*. Mankato, MN: Heinemann-Raintree, 2014.

Kopp, Megan. *Natural Disasters: Tsunamis*. New York: Weigl, 2014.

Markovics, Joyce L. *Tsunami*. New York: Bearport, 2014.

Winchester, Simon. *When the Earth Shakes: Earthquakes, Volcanoes, and Tsunamis*. Washington, DC: Smithsonian, 2015.

WEB SITES

Geography for Kids: Tsunamis
http://kidsgeo.com/geography-for-kids/0146B-tsunamis.php
This Web site contains facts and a video about how tsunamis form.

National Oceanic and Atmospheric Administration: Tsunami
http://www.education.noaa.gov/Ocean_and_Coasts/Tsunami.html
This Web site provides lessons, activities, and facts about tsunamis.

Weird Science Kids: Make a Tsunami!
http://weirdsciencekids.com/TsunamiSimulationExperiment.html
This Web site provides a tsunami simulation experiment.

GLOSSARY

buoy (BOO-ee) a floating object in the water

deflect (DUH-flekt) to cause to change direction

displaces (diss-PLAYSS-ez) moves something from its usual place

ecosystems (EE-koh-siss-tuhmz) communities of plants and animals in certain areas

friction (FRIK-shuhn) the force that slows objects down as they rub against each other

magma (MAG-muh) melted rock from beneath Earth's surface

run-up height (RUHN-uhp HIYT) the highest point a wave reaches onshore before it starts to go back

seismologists (SIZE-mah-low-jists) scientists who study earthquakes

subduction zone (sub-DUK-shun ZOHN) a place where the edge of a tectonic plate slides into the mantle beneath another plate

tectonic (tek-TON-ik) relating to the structure and processes of Earth's crust

wavelength (WAYV-length) the distance between one crest of a wave and the next

INDEX

[21ST CENTURY SKILLS LIBRARY]